MEXICAN COOKBOOK

Mexican Cookbook

By

Erna Fergusson

Illustrations by

Li Browne

*Nadie sabe lo que tiene la olla mas que la
cuchara que la menea.—No one knows
what's in the pot but the spoon
that stirs it*

UNIVERSITY OF NEW MEXICO PRESS

ALBUQUERQUE

Manufactured in the United States of America.
Library of Congress Catalog Card Number 46-214.
International Standard Book Number 0-8263-0035-9.

Foreword

Mexican food has, ever since the "American Occupation," been a part of the Southwestern diet. At first chile and beans and corn in many guises were all one could get. Later the deliciousness of slowly-cooked and richly condimented dishes won them fame among people who could not even pronounce their names. In every Southwestern town *tostadas* are served with cocktails, chile suppers are served regularly in many homes, and the family often goes out to a "chile joint," and the *tamale* vender with his tinkling bell and musical call moseys along the streets or lingers wherever people gather.

Now that everybody has been to the Southwest and even into Mexico, Mexican food has become a part of the national cuisine. Restaurants which prepare Mexican food correctly are demonstrating that much crude, hot food that used to pass as authentic lacks the subtlety of flavor characteristic of real Mexican cookery. The national palate is beginning to distinguish between a hot stew with chile dumped in and a smoothly blended dish of meat and spices; between heavy pancakes topped with a fried egg and a burning sauce, and a balanced combination of eggs, cheese, and chile on tender *tortillas*.

An all-inclusive Mexican cookbook would contain many recipes that call for tropical fruits and vegetables. The recipes in this book are limited to those which were in common use when the province of New Mexico was a part of the Republic of Mexico. They represent Mexican cookery that belongs to the United States.

Contents

Introduction

THE MEXICAN COOKBOOK has been out of print
for several years, but its friends continue to ask for
it. To a native New Mexican "chile food" is some-
thing he keeps on wanting even in a new world of
tightened geography and atomic bombs. New Mexicans proved that by writing home from earth's farthest
corners for chile and beans and blue corn meal and
the necessary herbs. In England they found *chile con
carne* almost warming enough to offset the climate;
on Pacific atolls they loved to sit on their heels around
a pot bubbling with succulent frijoles and smelling
just like home; and in the Philippines they could show a
trick or two to Spanish-speaking people who knew not
New Mexico's piquant food. Now that they are com-
ing back with brides, they think the girl from New
Zealand or Iceland, Italy or Scotland, should know how
to cook up a mess of beans for a hungry man.

So the little book comes out again, in a new
jacket and with new illustrations by a granddaughter of
New Mexico. It greets returning New Mexicans and
welcomes new New Mexicans who may find useful
hints here.

Since the book's first appearance it has become constantly clearer that in the old days every recipe had as many variations as there were cooks: a natural result of the fact that cookbooks were unknown. Some of these cooks made kindly comments on our recipes and offered new ones. In 1940, some of the original recipes were changed where it seemed that they might be made even easier to follow in a modern kitchen; and twelve new ones were included. These were offered by Miss Mela Sedillo and Señora Máxima Tafoya de Salazar. Señora Florinda Barela gave valuable advice and assistance in adapting the recipes. They were all tested again by Mrs. E. A. McDevitt as painstakingly as she tested the original ones when she was Miss Estelle Weisenbach.

Mexican Cookery

Now

MOST of these recipes were given me by Doña Lola Chaves de Armijo, who also helped with the menus.

With very few exceptions, these dishes date from the days when cooks were limited to what was raised in New Mexico and a few importations; and when all the work of preparing food was done in the home kitchens and *placitas*. All old and excellent cooks maintain that the full flavor of Mexican cookery depends upon doing everything as in the old days, when women worked slowly with their hands and with only the simplest equipment. Corn, they say, is never just right unless it is hulled and ground in the old way; and the proper blending of spices requires long and gentle simmering.

To an extent this is true, but Miss Estelle Weisenbach, a domestic science teacher who has tested all these recipes, finds them thoroughly practicable for a modern cook in a modern kitchen. Mechanical devices can lessen the strain on the human back. Commercial products may often be substituted for ingredients that call for laborious preparation. And all the ingredients may now be bought ready and correctly prepared.

3

These recipes were tested in a high altitude and a shorter cooking time may be allowed at sea level.

Each recipe will serve six people.

THEN

NOTHING more surely reflects the life of a people than what they ate and how they prepared it. When the railroad came to New Mexico, fifty years ago, it changed everything, even what went on in the kitchen. Imagine the difference when flour and meal could be ground in mills instead of on *metates;* when white sugar could be bought, and lemons and oranges; and machinery made ice; and there were iron stoves.

Before that, New Mexican cooks had to handle materials which came to them not in cellophane or glass, but in the rough. Great carcasses were dumped at their feet by the butchers who brought beef and mutton and pork. Hunters came in with buffalo "jerky" and the more delicate venison, birds, and fish. What the family could eat was used fresh. As there was no refrigeration, all the rest had to be dried. One woman might do that job and nothing else the whole year through. Another might understand the herbs which were used for seasoning and for medicine. From early spring until late fall she would watch for the exact moment to gather the leaves or blossoms or seeds which she dried and stored away. As fruits and vegetables ripened, they were eaten fresh or sun-dried for the winter by the expert at that job. By fall the rising tide of good things had filled the *placitas* with piles of parti-colored corn, trays of drying fruits, hanging bunches of grapes, and yellow pumpkins on sticks until they seemed to overflow in the brilliant strings of aromatic chile hanging from the roofs.

In the great kitchens all this food was cooked over open fires in iron or copper pots, or in the outdoor ovens still so generally used in New Mexico. Almost everything was cooked for hours, the sort of cooking that blends flavors until only an expert can tell what went into the dish. Apparently everything was done in the hardest possible way, but these methods were the result of conditions so primitive that we can scarcely believe them now. Corn and wheat were ground on *metates* because there were no mills. Chile likewise. Fruits were dried because there was no sugar for preserving.

Markets were two months' journey away, so the only importations were articles that could be kept indefinitely: coffee, sugar, chocolate, and spices, all from Mexico. As trade with "the States" developed, manufactured articles came from there until they gradually changed all of life. Nowadays the foreign importations are easier to get than the old-fashioned hand-ground meal or native herbs. At least one store in each New

Mexican town usually has these old things. Often one can also purchase *nixtamal,* the hominy called for in the recipes, or *masa,* the freshly ground meal.

The menus are based on meals as served at a gentleman's table before the general adoption of American ways. Then eating was a serious matter, interfered with only by famine, war, or Lent. The day began with a preliminary breakfast in bed; coffee or chocolate and sweet rolls. At nine o'clock came the real breakfast which included eggs or meat and more bread and coffee.

After that the *Señora* put in her heavy work of unlocking cupboards, storerooms, and chests; of dispensing food for the day; and of directing her servants. Naturally she felt fagged by eleven o'clock and ready for the *caldo colado* or clear soup, which came as a pick-me-up at that hour. Probably the gentlemen came in then from their business of ordering the outdoor work, and children escaped from tutors and governesses.

At noon formal dinner was served; a heavy soup, meats and vegetables, and desserts. The service in a wealthy family was of silver: platters, plates, and goblets. As there were no knives, the food was prepared in such a way that it could be managed with the silver forks and spoons. In a typical menu there were several meats and only one vegetable, various health rules not having been discovered. Beans and rice took the place of potatoes, which were neither raised nor imported. Salad was unusual. Wine or beer was served. Water was anathema—it was used for irrigation, washing, and religious purposes, never for drinking.

After this meal, one could indulge in the *siesta,* and come up refreshed for chocolate and more sweet cakes at four o'clock. Supper, at half past six, was a simple meal: chicken or spare ribs, fresh or dried vegetables according to the season, and corn meal dishes at any time.

By substituting supper menus for lunch and using less meat and more vegetables, and by the addition of salads, very satisfactory modern menus can be adapted from the old ones.

CHILE
CORN
FRUITS
SPICES
SOUPS

Chile

GREEN CHILE should be plucked when fully matured, but just before it turns red.

Wash and dry the pods and toast on top of the stove turning as they begin to blister. When the skin is evenly blistered and puffed away from the pulp, lay the pods on a cloth, sprinkle with water, and cover with another cloth to steam. The skins may then be pulled off and seeds removed.

Fresh green chile is often served in this way with meat or eggs.

To dry for winter use, lay in the shade, as the direct rays of the sun destroy the color. Turn often. When thoroughly dry, store in sacks. Before using, soak in warm water for half an hour, and mash into a pulp.

Remember that seeds are the hottest part and be guided accordingly.

Commercial canned chile may be substituted in equal proportions, though it has more bite than flavor, and the best of real chile is its flavor.

RED CHILE is never used fresh except when prepared in the same way as dried green chile. It is dried in the sun, hanging against the houses in the heavy *ristras,* which make such a brilliant color note in the fall.

To prepare either fresh or dried red chile, wash, break off the stems, and remove as many seeds as possible. Put to boil in cold water, and allow to boil slowly, moving the pods about in the water, but taking care not to break or mash them. Forty-five minutes to an hour's boiling is usually enough to let the skin slip easily. If the small end of the pod is pressed the pulp and seeds come out of the stem end readily. Rub through a colander to remove the remaining skin and seeds.

Boil for about 15 minutes in water in which the pods are boiled, and salt to taste. The final consistency should be that of a thick gravy. Twelve pulps make about a cup. This pulp should be made fresh every time, as it molds readily.

Chile must be handled very lightly, as it will burn the hands.

In all recipes, the best results are obtained by using this pulp, whether made from "outdoor" chile, or from commercial evaporated chile. Chile powder may be used, but the flavor is never as delicate.

In all recipes marked with an asterisk (*), for 1 cup chile pulp may be substituted 6 tablespoons chile powder and 1 tablespoon flour mixed with enough water to make a paste the consistency of a thick jam. Its ardors may be mitigated by using less chile and more flour.

CHILE SAUCE

1 cup of chile pulp or 4 to 6 tablespoons chile powder mixed with 1 tablespoon of flour

2 tablespoons of fat
1 small onion, chopped
1 clove of garlic, chopped
½ teaspoon salt

1 pinch *orégano*

Fry the onion and garlic in the fat, add salt and *orégano,* and chile pulp or chile powder and flour. Add enough water to make a thin gravy, and boil 20 minutes. If a milder sauce is wanted, add a beaten egg just before removing from the fire, or use more flour and less chile powder.

It is claimed for chile that "it protects against colds and malaria, it aids digestion, it clarifies the blood, it develops robustness and resistance to the elements; it even acts as a stimulant to the romantically inclined."

Corn

NIXTAMAL or HOMINY

To Hull

1 quart unslaked lye or wood ashes   1 gallon water

Boil about half an hour, then stir until it stops bubbling. Strain and add as much shelled corn as the water will cover. Boil slowly until the hulls slip easily between the fingers. Pour into a colander to drain. Wash in several waters until the taste of lye is gone.

This is *nixtamal* which may be used fresh, dried for storing, or ground to make *masa*. Ideally corn should be prepared fresh for every dish, but as the recipes indicate, ready-ground corn meal may be substituted for *masa*.

The best corn meal is the blue corn meal now generally available. It is prepared by washing and sun-drying the kernels, roasting them in adobe ovens, and grinding. The meal ground on *metates* or in old-fashioned watermills seems to have a better flavor than the product of modern machinery. And who knows why?

15

CHICOS
To Preserve and Dry

Leave the husks on fresh sweet corn and boil 30 minutes or roast in the oven 1 hour. When dry, strip the husks back, remove silk, and hang by the husks in a suitable storage place.

Shell the corn from the cob as needed. Use the whole grain or grind or crush it. If the whole grain is used, it must be soaked overnight. If crushed, soak in cold water for 1 hour before cooking.

This dry corn may be substituted for fresh corn in soups, stews, etc.

ATOLE
(Corn Gruel)

¾ cups blue corn meal or commercial meal toasted in the oven to a delicate brown

3 cups boiling water
1 teaspoon salt

Add enough cold water to the meal to moisten well (¼ to ½ cup), then stir in the boiling water to which salt has been added. Stir until smooth. Cook directly over the flame for 10 minutes, stirring constantly.

Serve with enough hot milk to make a thin gruel.

16

Fruits

WITH the exception of a few native berries, all fruits were brought into New Mexico by Spanish monks. Every mission and every home was surrounded by vineyards and orchards, watered by brown ditches and generally tended by Indian converts. A part of the routine of every household was the gathering and preserving or drying of fruit.

Peaches and *Apricots* were broken open, stoned, and laid to dry on scrubbed boards in the sun. This process retains all the natural sugar.

Apples were cored, quartered, and treated in the same way.

Prunes were dried whole.

Grapes were hung on hoops or poles, dried in the sun, and moved, pole or hoop and all, to the storeroom. They were soaked in warm water to freshen before serving.

Pumpkins and *Melons* were quartered, seeded, stuck on sticks, and dried in the sun.

Spices

Orégano is wild marjoram. The leaf was dried in the air, powdered between the fingers, and stored in jars.

Culantro is coriander. The seed was gathered when ripe, dried, ground, and stored. It is potent, and a pinch is usually enough.

Anís is anise, but with a different pronunciation. The seeds were dried and stored.

Yerba Buena, wild mint, was strung, dried in the air, and moved to the storeroom shelf. The tender leaves were stripped from the stems and used for garnishing as well as flavoring.

Black sage grows wild in the high altitudes of New Mexico. The leaves were dried and stored.

Laurel, with the Spanish pronunciation, was grown in gardens for kitchen use. In recipes it generally appears as bay leaf.

Azafran, saffron, grows wild. It lacks the flavor of Spanish saffron and is used more for color than taste.

Chimajá is wild celery. Both root and leaf are used. The leaf should be dried like *orégano*. The root is chopped when fresh or dried and ground.

SPICES

Comino, the seed of a wild plant, is dried and used whole or crushed.

(All these herbs should be used sparingly as it is the almost undetectable flavor rather than outright taste which is desirable.)

Piloncillo is brown Mexican sugar. It is sold in *little pillars,* and should be used whenever possible. Ordinary brown sugar may be substituted, but it is not nearly so good.

Soups

CALDO COLADO
(Clear Soup)

BEFORE the days of refrigeration, only lamb was killed during the summer. It was butchered by removing the hind quarters, loin, and shoulder pieces from the backbone, which was used for soup.

For modern use:

1½ pounds lamb, preferably from the backbone
1½ to 2 quarts water   1 chopped onion
1½ teaspoon salt

Cover the bone with cold water, add onion and salt and simmer slowly 4 hours, adding more hot water if needed.

Serve with

1 chopped onion browned in lard
1 cup dry bread crumbs
1 pinch *orégano*

1 chile pulp with a few seeds
½ tablespoon chile powder

Brown all together and add to the *Caldo Colado* one minute before serving.

PUREE OF CORN OR PEAS

1 quart of fresh corn or peas, or 1 can of corn or peas	2 tablespoons butter
	2 tablespoons flour
	2 cups scalded milk
2 cups cold water	1 teaspoon salt
1 chopped onion	¼ teaspoon chile
1 clove of garlic	1 pinch *culantro*

Cook corn or peas, onion and garlic in water until tender. Rub through a colander. Thicken with butter and flour, add milk just before serving. Season with salt, chile, and *culantro*.

If peas are used, add 1 teaspoon of sugar.

ALBÓNDIGAS SOUP

1 quart tomatoes	1 teaspoon salt

½ cup red chile pulp or 2 tablespoons chile powder

1 pinch *orégano*

Rub tomatoes through a colander and bring to a boil, adding enough water to make 2 quarts of liquid. Add chile pulp, salt, and *orégano* and boil down to 3 pints of liquid.   Add *albóndigas,* made as directed on page 34 and boil 1 hour.

Plain bean soup with no seasoning but salt may be substituted for this stock.

BEAN SOUP

1 pint *frijoles*
(only *frijoles*, Mexican
beans, should be used)
2 quarts cold water
1 sliced onion
2 cloves garlic

1 chile pulp, red or green,
or 1½ teaspoons chile
powder
1 tablespoon *orégano*
½ tablespoon salt

Soak the *frijoles* overnight in cold water, after picking them over carefully and washing well. In the morning, drain and put to cook in the cold water. Boil slowly from 4 to 6 hours, or all day, if possible. Add more boiling water as needed. When *frijoles* are half done, add salt. When tender, add onion, garlic, *orégano*, chile, and boil until all are tender. Rub through a colander and reheat, adding boiling water until the soup is the consistency of a purée.

Fifteen minutes before serving ¾ cup finely grated cheese may be added. Goat's milk cheese is best.

Serve with small cubes of bread fried in deep fat.

ENTREES
MEATS AND POULTRY

Entrees

GREEN CHILE SANDWICHES

12 green chile pods,   ½ teaspoon salt
   prepared as directed ⅛ teaspoon each black
¼ teaspoon finely   sage and *culantró*
   chopped garlic

Add the seasoning to the mashed chile and spread the paste between slices of bread covered with mayonnaise. Mayonnaise is better than butter because it mitigates the burning of the chile. Canned green chile may be used.

ENCHILADAS

Tortillas, made according to recipe, on page 87. Serve with the following sauce.

2 tablespoons lard	4 tablespoons olive oil
1 large onion, chopped	1 teaspoon *orégano*
3 cloves garlic, chopped	½ tablespoon salt
4 cups chile pulp	½ pound cheese
2 tablespoons vinegar	1 pint ripe olives

Brown onion and garlic in hot lard. Add chile pulp, vinegar, olive oil, *orégano,* and salt. Cook for at least 30 minutes; longer is better. While sauce is cooking, grate cheese, pit and chop olives.

Heat lard in a large skillet as for deep fat frying. When boiling hot, dip *tortillas* in fat, then in the hot sauce, and lay on a platter. Cover each *tortilla* with grated cheese and olives and add another until there are four in a pile. Top pile with a fried egg, and set in oven until cheese is melted.

A dish of chopped onions and a dish of chile sauce should be placed on the table when *enchiladas* are served. *Frijoles* complete the meal.

CHAUQUEHUE

1 ½ cups blue or toasted   1 ½ teaspoons salt
    corn meal   1 tablespoon fat
5 cups boiling water

Follow directions for *Atole*. Add lard after boiling water has been stirred in, cook slowly until stiff, about 20 minutes.

Chaquehue is thicker than *atole*. Serve with chile or spare ribs in place of potatoes or rice.

OSTIONES
(Oysters)

This recipe comes from Mexico where **very** fine oysters are found in the Gulf of California.

1 serving

4 to 6 oysters   salt and pepper
1 tablespoon butter   4 strips green chile
1 pinch *orégano*

Put the oysters into a buttered *cazuela* or ramekin. Add butter, sprinkle with salt and pepper and lay the strips of chile on top. If oysters are dry, oyster liquor or water may be added.

Bake in hot oven until the oysters become plump and edges begin to curl (about 10 minutes).

Just before serving place croutons of bread fried in butter on top.

CHILES RELLENOS

1 pound round steak	½ teaspoon salt
2 tablespoons lard	½ cup seedless raisins
½ cup sugar	6 green chiles, chopped
¼ teaspoon cloves	½ cup vinegar or red wine
¼ teaspoon cinnamon	3 eggs

Boil round steak and grind. Brown in hot lard. Add sugar, spices, salt, raisins, chiles, and liquid. Mix thoroughly and mould into egg-shaped croquettes.

Beat egg whites very stiff. Add yolks and beat. Roll each croquette in flour, then in the beaten egg and fry in deep fat.

2 cups of dry native mushrooms may be substituted for the steak. *(Boil mushrooms about 10 minutes, chop, or grind.)

*This is an excellent variation for Lent.

CHILES RELLENOS CON QUESO
(Chiles Stuffed with Cheese)

12 green chiles, seeded   6 tablespoons hot water
2 pounds cheese   flour enough to make a
6 eggs   thin batter
½ teaspoon salt

Cream the cheese and fill the chiles with it.

Beat the eggs to a froth, add water, salt, and flour to make a thin batter, about ½ cup. Dip each chile into the batter, and fry in deep fat until a deep golden brown. Drain chiles and set aside where they will stay hot.

Prepare the following sauce:

2 cups fresh stewed tomatoes   3 tablespoons butter
   or 1 can tomatoes   3 tablespoons flour
¼ teaspoon *orégano*   1 teaspoon salt
1 onion, chopped   ⅛ teaspoon pepper
2 cloves garlic

Cook tomatoes and *orégano* for 15 minutes, and rub through a colander. Brown onions and garlic in butter, dip them out and brown flour in the same butter. Stir in onion and garlic, tomato pulp, salt and pepper. Cook for 3 minutes and pour over the stuffed chiles. Serve hot. The sauce may be strained if desired.

CHICHARRONES
(Cracklings)

This is the fat cut from under the skin of the hog. The best comes from the part where the bacon is cut.

To prepare, cut into small pieces and cook slowly in the oven, stirring often, until all the lard is rendered out and the *chicharrones* are a delicate brown. Then strain.

The may be served cold lightly salted as an hors d'oeuvre.

MACARONI CON CHILE

2 cups boiled macaroni
1 onion, chopped
1½ teaspoons salt
⅛ teaspoon *comino*
1 red or green chile pulp
2 cups tomato pulp
½ cup grated cheese

Brown onion in fat. Mix all ingredients with macaroni, pour into greased baking dish, cover with grated cheese, and bake in moderate oven about thirty minutes.

33

ALBONDIGAS

1 pound beef	1 clove garlic, chopped
½ pound pork	1 pinch each black sage
1 slice bread	ground mint, and pepper
1 egg	1 teaspoon salt
1 onion	1 tomato

⅛ teaspoon *culantro*

Grind meat together, mix with bread, which has been soaked in water and squeezed dry. Add egg and seasoning. Mix well and mold into balls the size of walnuts. Brown 1 chopped onion in 2 tablespoons fat. Remove onion and brown meat balls. Add onion, 1 mashed tomato, spices as above, and 4 to 6 cups of boiling water. Simmer slowly for 1½ hours.

BURRITOS
(Little Burros)

Mix *tortillas* according to recipe on page 87, but mold them thicker than usual. Make a depression in the middle of each and fill with *chicharrones,* made according to recipe on page 33, and chopped. Bake in a moderate oven.

Meats and Poultry

LA OLLA PODRIDA
(Savory Pot)

½ pound each pork, chicken, veal, beef, all cubed

1½ teaspoons salt

⅛ teaspoon each cinnamon, all-spice, nutmeg, cloves

½ teaspoon pepper

1 wine-glass sherry

1 pinch *chimajá*

Omit salt if salted sherry is used

Add seasoning to meat and mix well. Line a greased baking pan with pastry rolled ⅜ inch thick. Pour in meat, dredge with flour, and add water to cover. Cover with top crust, bake in hot oven 12 minutes and continue baking in slow oven 2 to 3 hours. When meat is done, lift top crust and add sherry.

For pastry, use recipe for *pastel* on page 85.

SPANISH ROAST

1½ pounds round steak,   1 cup flour
    cut 2 inches thick   4 ripe tomatoes, cubed
1 sliced onion   1 green chile pulp
½ teaspoon salt   ¼ teaspoon pepper
     1 pinch *chimajá*

Pound flour into steak and season. Brown quickly on both sides in 3 tablespoons of very hot fat. Add tomatoes, onion, chile, and about two cups of hot water. Cover and bake in a moderate oven until tender, about 1½ hours.

SPANISH MEAT LOAF

1 pound hamburger or
  1 pound shoulder beef
¾ pound pork
1 chopped onion
½ clove garlic
1 green chile pulp or
  1 canned green chile

¼ teaspoon pepper
1 egg
1 cup bread crumbs
¼ cup of milk
1 teaspoon salt
3 hard-boiled eggs
1 pinch *chimajá*

1 pinch mint

Add seasoning to ground meat, mix well, add crumbs, egg well-beaten, and milk. Cut off the ends of each hard-boiled egg and fit them together to make a center for the loaf. Mold the meat around the eggs to make a round loaf.

Make a biscuit dough as follows:

2 cups flour
2 tablespoons fat
1 teaspoon salt

4 teaspoons baking
  powder
¾ cup sweet milk

Mix and sift flour, baking powder, and salt. Cut in the fat. Add milk gradually to make a soft dough. Place dough on lightly floured board, roll to about one-third inch thickness, and roll around the meat roll.

37

Bake in a quick oven for 12 minutes, cover, and finish baking in a moderate oven for 2 hours. Serve hot.

When sliced at the table it shows a yellow and white center to each slice of meat.

TEMOLE DE CHILE VERDE
(Stew of Green Chile)

1 pound round steak cut in small cubes
1 tablespoon flour
2 tablespoons lard
1 small onion, chopped

4-6 green chiles, chopped
1 clove garlic, chopped fine
2 cups boiling water
1 teaspoon salt
⅛ teaspoon pepper

Sprinkle steak with flour and brown steak and onion in hot lard. Add chiles, garlic, water, and seasoning. Simmer about 30 minutes. If necessary, add more boiling water.

A small can of tomatoes may be added.

CHILE CON CARNE
(Meat with Chile)

2 pounds mutton or beef
1 pound fresh pork
4 cloves garlic, chopped
2 tablespoons lard or
   drippings
3 bay leaves
1 quart ripe tomatoes or
   1 large can tomatoes

1 onion, chopped
1 cup chile pulp or
   6 tablespoons chile
   powder
1 tablespoon *orégano*
1 tablespoon salt
1 pint ripe olives
1 teaspoon *comino*

Cut the meat into small cubes. Brown onion and garlic in fat, add meat. Cover and steam thoroughly. Rub tomatoes through colander, add to meat, stir in chile pulp, and cook for 20 minutes. Add seasoning and cook slowly for 2 hours. Cut olives from the pits, add and cook for another ½ hour.

Serve with *frijoles*.

If chile powder is used, mix with 1 tablespoon flour, stir into fat in which onion and garlic were browned, stir until smooth. Then add meat and proceed as above.

BOILED DINNER

Mutton was and still is the meat most generally used by Mexican housewives. It was roasted in outdoor ovens or boiled with enough seasoning to disguise the fact that it was usually served very fresh. The modern housewife may get the very flavor of the old dish with the best cold storage mutton.

2 pounds lean mutton	1 red chile pulp or
½ tablespoon salt	½ tablespoon chile powder*
1 solid head cabbage	1 bunch each of small
3 large tomatoes	beets, turnips, onions,
3 potatoes	carrots
2 sour apples	1 tablespoon *orégano*

Remove bones, roll and tie meat so it will retain its shape while cooking. Put into a kettle of cold water and bring to a boil. Add vegetables; cabbage should be tied in a cheesecloth bag; beets should not be peeled. Vegetables must all be thoroughly cooked.

An hour before serving add the apples, chile, and tomatoes, each tied in a separate cheesecloth bag. Also salt, *orégano* and Worcestershire Sauce. Peel beets before serving. The whole dish should simmer at least 3 hours.

* See page 12

CARNE DE MARRANO Y CHILE
(Pork with Chile)

1 leg of pork	⅛ teaspoon *culantro*
12 red chile pulp	⅛ teaspoon ground black
or 3 tablespoons chile	sage
powder	1 clove of garlic, chopped
½ teaspoon salt	

Add seasoning to chile pulp and rub together into a thick paste. Cut five or six holes in the meat and fill with the mixture. Plug holes with the meat again and roast in a slow oven, allowing 30 minutes for each pound. Half an hour before the meat is done, spread with the remaining paste and brown.

Chile powder mixed with seasoning and water may be substituted for chile paste.

CARNE ADOBADA
(Spiced Meat)

1 pork loin, cut into strips   4 cloves garlic mashed
12 red chile pulp and seeds   1 teaspoon salt
   or substitute*   ⅛ teaspoon *orégano*

Add seasoning to chile pulp. Soak meat in this mixture. Three minutes is usually enough, but the longer it stays the stronger it gets. Take strips out and hang in a cool place to dry. Serve roasted or fried.

If chile powder is used, add water enough to make a paste.

* *See page 12*

POSOLE (1)
(Hog and Hominy)

2 pounds pork, cubed
2 onions, chopped
1 bay leaf
1 tablespoon fat
½ teaspoon *orégano*

1 cup red chile pulp or
4-6 tablespoons chile
powder
1 cup *nixtamal* (hominy)
1 teaspoon salt

Fry onions in fat, add pork and blend. Add *nixtamal* or hominy, chile, and seasoning. Add hot water and simmer until pork is thoroughly tender, about 4 hours. Serve steaming hot. If chile powder is used, mix with 1 tablespoon of flour and stir into fat.

If canned hominy is used, cook pork first until almost done before adding hominy. Then simmer until done.

POSOLE (2)

6 pigs feet
1 onion chopped
seeds of 4 chiles
1 clove garlic chopped
1 tablespoon fat
½ teaspoon *orégano*

12 red chile pulp or
    4 to 6 tablespoons chile
    powder
1 teaspoon salt
1 quart *nixtamal* or
    canned hominy

Tie pigs feet in a cheesecloth bag and cook until tender. Brown onion and garlic in fat, add to the pigs feet. Then add chile, *orégano*, salt, and hominy. Simmer until hominy is done.

ROAST SUCKLING PIG

Prepare pig for roasting. Rub inside with a mixture of salt and pepper and stuff with the following dressing:

2 loaves stale bread	2½ teaspoon salt
1 onion, chopped	½ teaspoon sage
1 clove garlic, chopped	½ teaspoon pepper
1 cup seeded raisins	generous pinch *chimajá* or
1 pinch mint	¼ teaspoon celery salt

Remove crust from bread, slice, moisten in hot chicken broth and squeeze out surplus moisture. Fry in fat. When the mass leaves the pan easily, add other ingredients and mix well. Stuff pig, sew together and roast until well done. Do not baste, but occasionally prick the skin so it will not blister. When pig is done, pour a glass of red wine over it and put a red apple in its mouth.

This dressing may be used also with roast turkey.

COCIDO
(Stew)

In Spain, in Mexico, probably in every Spanish-speaking country, *cocido* was the most important dish. It is generous as it is soup, meat, and vegetables, and it is meant to last several meals, getting more savory with each reheating. "And what they could not eat that night, the queen next morning fried."

1 pound fresh pork	1 bunch of carrots
2 pounds beef	2 onions
3 slices bacon	1 stalk of celery
2 corn on the cob	2 summer squash
2 Irish potatoes	½ head of cabbage
2 sweet potatoes	1 apple
1 cup of *garbanzos* prepared as on page 63	1 pear
	1 pinch *comino*
1 generous pinch *orégano*	1 teaspoon salt
1 turnip	

Cut the meat in large cubes and wash the other things, but do not peel them. Start with the meat, *garbanzos* tied in a cheesecloth bag, corn cut into small lengths, potatoes, cabbage, and turnips, covered with water. Later add the other vegetables, and last the fruit, all whole. Then add salt, *orégano* and *comino*.

It should simmer slowly for 3 to 4 hours. If the fruit gets done, take it out.

The soup may be served first and then the rest.

For the second day's serving, cut corn from the cob, run everything through a meat grinder, and fry in lard until it leaves the pan.

For both servings, two sauces may be offered.

Sweet Sauce

1 onion	2½ tablespoons sugar
2 tablespoons lard	½ teaspoon salt
2 tomatoes	3 tablespoons vinegar

Chop the onion very fine and fry in lard until it begins to brown. Add tomatoes and seasoning and fry until it leaves the pan. Serve hot.

Piquant Sauce

½ onion	½ teaspoon salt
2 tomatoes	3 tablespoons vinegar
2 pods red chile pulp	1 tablespoon of oil

Chop the onion, mash the tomatoes, add salt, chile, vinegar, and oil. Beat until smooth. Serve cold.

ASADITO
(Little Roast)

2 pounds veal, lamb, or mutton ribs

2 tablespoons flour

3 tablespoons lard or fat from the meat

1 small can tomatoes

1 onion

1½ teaspoons salt

⅛ teaspoon pepper

2 tablespoons rice

3 cups boiling water

Cut ribs in small pieces, sprinkle with flour and brown in hot lard or in fat cut from the meat. Add water, tomatoes, and onion cut small.

Simmer 1 hour, then add rice and seasoning and simmer another hour, or until the meat is tender.

Instead of rice, *chicos* or green corn cut from the cob may be used.

Chicos should be partially cooked separately and added when the meat has cooked an hour. Green corn requires only 30 minutes of cooking.

TAMALE PASTEL
(Tamale Pie)

1 onion, chopped
1 clove garlic, chopped
1 tablespoon lard
2 cups boiled pork, cubed
½ cup red chile pulp or 2/3 tablespoon chile powder
1 cup ripe olives, pitted and chopped
⅛ teaspoon *culantro*
1 tablespoon lard
1 teaspoon salt
1 teaspoon Worcestershire Sauce
1 cup fresh tomatoes, mashed or 1 cup canned tomatoes
½ cup meat stock
2 cups *masa* or blue corn meal
2 teaspoons salt
6 cups boiling water or meat stock

Brown onions and garlic in lard; add pork, chile, olives, seasonings, tomatoes, and meat stock. Simmer 10 minutes.

Stir cornmeal into boiling salted water or stock, add lard and cook over low heat about 15 minutes, stirring frequently. Line sides and bottom of baking dish with mush. Pour in meat mixture and cover with remaining mush. Bake slowly until done, about 1 hour.

If *masa* is used, less water is needed in preparing the mush.

POLLO CON ARROZ
(Chicken with Rice)

1 chicken
½ tablespoon salt
3 tablespoons fat

1 onion, chopped
1 clove garlic, chopped
1 cup uncooked rice
pinch saffron powder

Dress, clean, and cut chicken as for frying. Cover with boiling water and boil for 15 minutes. Then add salt. Heat fat, add onion and garlic, stir in rice and cook until well mixed, but not browned. When chicken is tender, add this mixture and simmer until rice is done. Add saffron powder just before serving.

POLLO RELLENO
(Stuffed Chicken)

1 chicken	pinch cloves
½ tablespoon salt	½ teaspoon salt
1 pound round steak	¼ teaspoon cinnamon
½ cup seeded raisins	3 tablespoons fat

1 pinch *chimajá*

Cover chicken with boiling water, boil 15 minutes and add salt. Boil slowly until almost tender. Boil round steak until done. Put through a chopper and add raisins, salt, *chimajá*, cloves, and cinnamon. Heat the fat and brown this mixture in it. Stuff the chicken and bake until tender. Baste with the meat stock, spiced with cinnamon and cloves.

CHICKEN STEWED IN SHERRY

1 chicken	1 red or green chile or ½
2 onions, chopped	tablespoon chile powder
3 cloves garlic, chopped	1 pint ripe olives,
2 bay leaves	chopped
½ tablespoon salt	1 pint sherry
1 teaspoon *orégano*	4 tablespoons flour

Dress, clean, and cut chicken as for frying. Cover with boiling water and boil 15 minutes. Add onion, garlic, bay leaves, salt, and *orégano,* and boil slowly. One hour before chicken is done, add chile, olives, and sherry, and simmer until tender. If salted sherry is used, omit salt. Thicken gravy with flour diluted in enough water to pour easily. Boil 5 minutes. Serve with Spanish rice. Rabbit may be used.

EGGS
VEGETABLES
SALADS

Eggs

POACHED EGGS IN CHILE

3 cups water
8 green chiles, mashed
1 onion, chopped
1 clove garlic, chopped
1 pinch each *culantro,* black sage, and mint
1 teaspoon salt

Combine ingredients in a shallow pan and boil slowly until onion and garlic are cooked and the liquid has boiled down to one cup. Reduce the heat until the mixture stops bubbling. Break each egg separately into a saucer and slip gently into the mixture, which should not be boiling. Cook until the egg-white is firm and a film forms on the yolk. The mixture may be served as a sauce.

SPANISH OMELET

6 eggs	¼ teaspoon pepper
6 tablespoons hot water	3 tablespoons butter
¾ teaspon salt	

Beat eggs lightly, just enough to blend yokes and whites. Add water and seasoning. Melt butter in hot omelet pan and let it run over the bottom and sides of the pan. Pour in the mixture and cook slowly. As it cooks, prick with a fork so the egg on top will run under the sides. When evenly cooked, increase the heat so the omelet will brown underneath. Fold and serve on a hot platter with the following sauce:

8 large tomatoes, cubed	5 tablespoons fat
4 onions, chopped	1 cup green chile pulp
1 clove garlic, chopped	pinch *culantro*
⅛ teaspoon black sage	1 teaspoon salt

Cook tomatoes slowly for 10 minutes. Fry onion and garlic in hot fat. Combine all ingredients and simmer for 3 hours, adding hot water as necessary. Pour over omelet, or fill ends of platter with sauce just before serving.

TORTA DE HUEVO
(Egg Fritter)

3 eggs
2 teaspoons flour
1 pinch mint

½ teaspoon salt
½ teaspoon baking
  powder

1 pinch *orégano*

Beat whites stiff, add yolk, and beat again. Stir flour, spices, baking powder and salt lightly into eggs. Drop by teaspoonfuls into deep fat and fry. Drain and serve with chile sauce.

HUEVOS CON HONGOS
(Eggs with Mushrooms)

½ cup mushrooms, fresh
  or canned
1½ tablespoons butter or
  drippings
1 onion, chopped
6 tablespoons milk

1 green chile pulp
½ teaspoon salt
6 eggs
3 tablespoons of butter
  or drippings
1 pinch *orégano*

Clean mushrooms, remove stems and scrape. Peel caps and cube. Heat fat, add mushrooms, and cook until tender, about 10 minutes. Add several tablespoons hot water if necessary. Fry onion and chile in butter until tender, and add mushrooms. Beat eggs slightly, add salt, *orégano,* and milk, scramble with onion, chile, and mushrooms.

Vegetables

FRIJOLES
(Beans)

2 cups *frijoles* (Mexican beans)

1/3 pound salt pork
1 pinch *orégano*

Pick over beans carefully and soak overnight. Drain and cover with fresh cold water. Add salt pork and *orégano,* boil slowly until tender, 4 to 6 hours. If possible, cook at simmering temperature all day. As water boils away, add boiling water; never cold.

Frijoles may be served just as they come from the pot. If a larger quantity is cooked, they may be used the second day with chile.

This quantity will make ten servings.

FRIJOLES CON CHILE
(Beans with Chile)

Heat two tablespoons lard or drippings to the bubbling point in a large iron skillet. Add cooked beans, prepared according to the above recipe, drain off liquor, and mash beans into the hot grease. Add liquor enough to cook for one hour, very slowly. Then add chile sauce, prepared as follows.

One-half cup grated cheese may be added to the beans just before serving.

Chile Sauce for Frijoles

1 tablespoon fat
1 large onion, chopped
3 cloves garlic, chopped
2 tablespoons olive oil
½ teaspoon salt

¼ teaspoon *orégano*
1 tablespoon vinegar
½ cup chile pulp or 2 tablespoons chile powder

1 cup hot water

Heat fat and cook onion and garlic slowly in the hot fat. Add olive oil, seasoning, vinegar, chile pulp, and water. Simmer for ½ hour. Add to beans and serve.

If a thicker sauce is desired, add 1 tablespoon flour to the mixture before liquid is added, and stir until smooth.

A milder sauce may be prepared by using all the above ingredients except the chile pulp and water. For these, substitute:

2 to 3 tablespoons chile powder   ½ tablespoon flour

1 cup tomatoes

½ cup stock or water

Add chile powder, flour, and seasoning to hot fat in which onion and garlic have been cooked. Stir until smooth. Add meat stock or water, tomatoes, oil, and vinegar. Simmer for ½ hour.

CHICOS CON FRIJOLES
(A Southwestern Succotash)

½ cup *chicos*
1 ½ cups *frijoles*

1 tablespoon lard, drippings, or small piece of salt pork

salt

Wash *chicos* and *frijoles* and soak overnight. Drain and cover with fresh, cold water.

Add lard and boil slowly until tender, 4-6 hours. Season to taste.

FRIJOLES REFRITOS
(Fried Beans)

Prepare as for *Frijoles con Chile* but without the chile sauce. Or use your left-over beans this way.

Heat fat in a deep skillet and when very hot test with a sprinkling of flour. When flour browns, put in your beans and fry until the beans form a mass which leaves the side of the pan. Mold in a long roll and serve hot.

GARBANZOS
(Chick Peas)

There are several varieties. Most require only an overnight soaking before cooking. If the skins are heavy it is advisable to boil in water with a teaspoon of soda until skins loosen, about 5 minutes. Remove from fire and rub between the hands in cold water to remove skins. Cover with cold water and cook until tender.

1 cup *garbanzos* or dried peas	1 onion, chopped
	½ cup red chile pulp
1 teaspoon salt	1 pinch *culantro*

Let peas stand overnight in cold water to cover. Bring to a boil, drain, and cover with fresh water. Add salt and *culantro* and boil 1 hour, or until tender.

Fry the onion in salt pork or bacon fat. Mash the peas lightly, add the onion and chile and reheat.

Serve as a vegetable.

BAKED GARBANZOS

2 pounds *garbanzos*   2 tablespoons flour
¼ pound butter   3 eggs
Salt and pepper to taste   1 pinch *culantro*

Prepare *garbanzos* as directed on page 63, boiling until tender. Then mash or press through a potato ricer. Stir in the flour, the yolks of eggs, lightly beaten, and seasoning. Add whites of eggs, beaten stiff.

Butter a baking dish, and dust with flour. Put lumps of butter on the bottom. Then pour in the mixture in layers with lumps of butter between and on top. Bake in a moderate oven 30 minutes. Serve as a vegetable.

By adding 1 cup of crushed *piloncillo* or brown sugar, this dish makes a satisfactory dish for dessert.

RICE

1 cup rice   3 cups boiling water
1 teaspoon salt

Wash rice and soak in cold water 1 hour. Boil water in upper part of double boiler, add salt and rice, slowly. Cook directly over flame for 5 minutes. Steam in double boiler 45 minutes or until soft.

The rice should be very dry when done. If it is not, stir lightly with a fork and allow to steam dry.

Mold in a dish and garnish with slices of hard-boiled eggs.

ARROZ
(Rice)

¾ cup rice   2¼ cups boiling water
¾ teaspoon salt

Follow directions for cooking rice. When almost done, add:

1 teaspoon sugar   ½ cup seeded raisins, chopped
1 tablespoon butter   ½ cup almonds, chopped

Finish cooking until rice is soft. Serve as a vegetable.

MEXICAN RICE

½ cup rice   4 cups boiling soup stock
2 tablespoons fat   ½ teaspoon salt
1 large onion, chopped   4 large ripe tomatoes
                3 red chiles, mashed

Wash rice and drain. Heat fat. Add rice and stir until brown. Add onion and brown. Rub tomatoes through a colander. To the rice and onion, add boiling soup stock, tomatoes, salt, chile. Simmer until rice is soft.

After rice and onion are brown, the dish may be cooked in a double boiler,

QUELITES
(Lamb's Quarters)

2 pounds *quelites*
1 tablespoon fat

1 onion, chopped
1 green chile, mashed

Carefully pick over *quelites*. Drop into boiling salted water and cook until tender. Drain well.

Brown onion and chile in fat. Add to *quelites*.

One cup cooked *frijoles* may be added.

Garden spinach may be substituted for *quelites*.

QUELITES CON CHILE

1 onion, chopped
1 red chile pulp

a few chile seeds
1 tablespoon fat

2 pounds *quelites*

Fry onions and chile in fat. Add to uncooked *quelites*. Add water and salt, and cook slowly until tender.

1 tablespoon chile powder may be substituted for the pulp and seeds.

STEAMED SQUASH

Cut a ripe summer squash into pieces, but do not remove the seeds or fiber. Steam until soft.

Serve with *piloncillo* and cream. Brown sugar may be substituted for *piloncillo*.

This is served as a supper dish.

ELEGANTE
(Chile and Squash)

2 pounds summer squash cubed	1 small onion, chopped
½ cup green corn	½ clove garlic, chopped
1 small green chile pulp	pinch *culantro*
1 large tomato, cubed	¼ teaspoon mint, chopped or ground
	1 teaspoon salt

Cut corn from the cob. Heat enough fat to cover the bottom of a pan, and add all ingredients. Cover and cook slowly about 10 minutes, stirring occasionally to prevent burning. Cover with milk and simmer about 1 hour.

¼ cup goat's milk cheese may be added just before serving. No other cheese should be substituted.

GREEN CORN WITH GREEN CHILE

3 cups green corn	3 tablespoons lard or
2-4 green chiles	olive oil
½-1 clove garlic,	¾ teaspoon salt
chopped fine	⅛ teaspoon pepper

Cut corn from the cob. Heat the fat in a frying pan. Add corn, chiles, and garlic. Cover and cook slowly until corn is tender, 10 to 15 minutes. Add seasoning. If corn seems too dry, add several tablespoons of boiling water while cooking.

MUSHROOMS

Native mushrooms should be cleaned, shredded or broken in pieces, covered with cheesecloth and dried in the sun for several days. They may then be kept for months in an air-tight container.

During Lent, mushrooms are often substituted for meat in such dishes as *Chiles Rellenos*. (See page 31)

They are also used with eggs. (See page 57)

FRIED MUSHROOMS

¼ pound dried mush-
rooms
1 clove garlic, chopped
fine

½ teaspoon salt
2 tablespoons lard or
olive oil
⅛ teaspoon pepper

Soak dry native or imported mushrooms in luke warm water until soft, about ½ hour. Drain, wash in several waters, and chop. Heat fat, add mushrooms, garlic, and seasoning. Cover and cook slowly until the mushrooms are tender, about 10 minutes.

One-half pound of fresh mushrooms may be used. Clean (peel if skins are shriveled), slice or chop.

Salads

SALADS were very little used; lettuce with a dressing of sugar and vinegar being the nearest approach. For modern menus, lettuce with French dressing or simple fruit salads of the tartest fruits make the best compliment to the Mexican dishes.

GUACAMOLE
(Avocado Salad)

3 avocados
1 large ripe tomato
1 cup chopped celery
½ teaspoon salt

1 red chile pulp or
1 teaspoon chile powder
1 tablespoon finely chopped onion

Mash avocados and chile, add remaining ingredients, mix with French dressing and serve on lettuce or chicory leaves.

Avocados mashed with garlic, chile paste or powder, lemon juice, and salt may be served with tostadas or any crisp crackers as hors d'ouvres.

AGUACATE
(Avocado)

3 avocados

1 clove garlic, finely chopped

1 cup olive oil

½ cup vinegar

Peel and slice avocado. Blend oil and vinegar and add garlic, and put avocados to soak overnight. Drain and serve on lettuce or chicory leaves with sharp French dressing.

French Dressing

6 tablespoons oil

2 tablespoons vinegar

½ teaspoon salt

¼ teaspoon paprika

Blend by shaking in a small jar.

If the flavor of garlic is desired, the oil and vinegar in which the avocados were soaked may be used in making the dressing.

SALSA DE CHILE VERDE
(Green Chile Sauce)

4 ripe tomatoes	1 clove garlic
6 green chiles	1 teaspoon salt
1 medium sized onion	⅛ teaspoon pepper

1 teaspoon vinegar

Mash garlic in a wooden salad bowl. Peel tomatoes. Remove the seeds and veins from the chiles. Chop chile and onion in salad bowl. Add tomatoes cut in small pieces, seasoning, and vinegar. Mix well and serve.

DESSERTS
BREADS
CAKES AND COOKIES

Desserts

ALMENDRADO
(Almond Pudding)

5 egg whites
1 cup granulated sugar
1 tablespoon gelatine
¼ cup cold water

1 cup boiling water
½ teaspoon almond
   extract
1 cup chopped almonds

Soak gelatine in cold water until it absorbs the water (about 5 minutes). Add the boiling water and dissolve thoroughly. Add sugar and stir until dissolved. Chill until it begins to stiffen, then beat until frothy.

Beat egg white stiff and add to gelatine when it begins to stiffen. Beat until the mixture is well blended. Add flavoring.

Pour into mold, alternating layer of mixture with chopped almonds. Set aside to stiffen. Serve with the following sauce.

Sauce

1 pint milk
5 egg yolks
¼ cup sugar

⅛ teaspoon salt
½ teaspoon vanilla
½ pint whipping cream

Scald the milk in a double boiler. Beat the eggs lightly, add sugar and salt, and pour slowly into this mixture the boiling milk. Cook in double boiler, stirring constantly, until the mixture thickens and coats the spoon. When cool, add vanilla and whipped cream.

ARROZ DULCE
(Rice Sweet)

¾ cup rice   2/3 cup sugar
4 cups milk   1 teaspoon vanilla
1 cup rich cream   ¼ teaspoon salt

Scald milk. Put the rice into a deep baking dish, cover with the hot milk, and bake in a moderate oven for 3 hours, or until the rice is soft. Stir occasionally during first hour to prevent sticking. If necessary, add more hot milk.

When almost done, add vanilla, sugar, and cream, and finish baking.

CAPIROTADA or TORREJAS (1)

2½ cups bread cubes   1 teaspoon cinnamon
1 egg   ¾ cup piñones
¼ cup sugar   ½ cup citron, finely chopped

(*Piñones* are the nuts of the *piñon* tree which grows very generally over New Mexico and Arizona. They may be bought in eastern markets.)

Brown bread cubes thoroughly in the oven. Separate the egg, beat the white until stiff, add the yoke, and beat again. Dip the bread cubes into the egg and fry in deep fat. Drain and pile on a hot dish. Sprinkle with sugar and cinnamon sifted together and add citron and *piñones*. Pour over this the following sauce, which must be hot when served.

Sauce

2 cups sugar   1 cup water
⅛ teaspoon cream of tartar   ½ teaspoon cinnamon

Combine the ingredients and heat gradually to the boiling point. Boil until the syrup threads.

CAPIROTADA (2)

4 cups water
2 cups crushed *piloncillo*
  or brown sugar
1 medium-sized onion
2 tomatoes

1 cup raisins
½ cup lard
½ cup butter
½ teaspoon cinnamon
1 loaf dry bread

1 cup grated cheese

Of the sugar and water, make a syrup about the consistency of maple syrup. When half done, add the onion and tomato, sliced. Strain. In a pudding dish put a layer of broken bread, then syrup, raisins, butter, and lard, until dish is filled. Bake about 45 minutes and serve hot.

SOPA
(Bread Pudding)

6 thin slices of bread,   1 cup seeded raisins
  toasted brown   1 cup grated cheese
6 thin slices of bread, fried in deep fat

In a deep buttered baking dish arrange a layer of toasted bread, a layer of fried bread, a layer of chopped raisins and grated cheese. Repeat. Add the following sauce.

Sauce

1 cup crushed piloncillo ½ teaspoon cinnamon
  or 1/3 brown sugar   2 cups water
            pinch cloves

Bring to a boil and pour on the bread in the dish. Add water if necessary to cover.

Bake in a slow oven until firm and well browned, about 1 hour.

CHONGOS
(Mexican Junket)

3 quarts milk   6 junket tablets
4 egg yolks   2 sticks of vanilla
            3 cups sugar

Beat egg yolks, add milk and sugar and mix well.
Add the junket tablets dissolved in warm water, then vanilla. Leave mixture in a warm place until it clabbers.

With a knife cut the curd into squares, and put on a very slow fire. When the whey separates increase the heat slightly, but it should cook very slowly for 2 to 3 hours. When the curds are a golden yellow and the syrup is the consistency of maple syrup, they are done.
Serve cold.

Chongos will keep for several days, getting better all the time.

ANTE
(Cake Pudding)

4 cups water	1 loaf dry plain cake
2 cups crushed *piloncillo*	1 cup raisins
or brown sugar	1 cup chopped *piñones*
yolks of 6 eggs	or blanched almonds
1/3 pound butter	½ teaspoon cinnamon

Of the sugar and water make a syrup the consistency of maple syrup. While still warm, beat in the 6 egg yolks well beaten and the butter. Stir until creamy. Cut the cake into squares and cover with the syrup. Allow it to soak overnight. Then arrange in a pudding dish in layers with the raisins, nuts, and dust with the cinnamon.

Serve cold.

NATILLAS
(Custard)

5 eggs

5 tablespoons granulated sugar

4 cups scalded milk

¼ teaspoon salt

¼ teaspoon cinnamon

3 tablespoons powdered sugar

1 teaspoon vanilla

Beat the yolks of the 5 eggs, and the whites of 2 eggs slightly. Add the granulated sugar, salt, and cinnamon and slowly pour in the scalded milk. Cook in a double boiler, stirring constantly until the mixture thickens and coats the spoon. Add the vanilla. Pour in a deep dish or custard cups.

Beat very stiff the whites of the remaining eggs. Add powdered sugar. Drop by spoonfuls on a pan of boiling water and steam until firm. Top the custard with meringue and dust with cinnamon.

PASTEL
(Pastry)

2 cups flour   ¾ teaspoon salt
½ teaspoon baking powder   2/3 cup butter or lard
        4 to 6 tablespoons cold water

Mix and sift dry ingredients. Cut in shortening until mixture is like coarse meal. Add only enough water to bind together. Roll out thin on a slightly floured board. Line pie pan and fill with a cooked fruit mixture. Cover with interlacing strips and bake in a quick oven for 10 minutes. Continue baking in a moderate oven for 20 minutes.

Pasteles are also made with all kinds of dried fruits. Prepare fruit as directed on page 98.
Anise may be sprinkled over just before serving.

PASTEL DE CALABAZA
(Pumpkin Pie)

2½ cups pumpkin   ½ teaspoon cinnamon
½ cup sugar   ⅛ teaspoon cloves
½ teaspoon salt   ⅛ teaspoon allspice
          ½ cup seeded raisins, chopped

Prepare pumpkin as for vegetable.   Mash the pulp, add sugar, salt, spices, and raisins.

Line pie pan with pastry and fill with mixture.   Bake 10 minutes in a quick oven until firm.

Canned pumpkin may be used, and ½ cup milk and 1 egg may be added to the above if desired.

Breads

TORTILLAS (1)
(With Corn Meal)

2 cups corn meal or *masa*   1 teaspoon salt
warm water

Mix corn meal or *masa* and salt.   If dry meal is used, add enough water to make a stiff dough, even the *masa* may require a little moisture.   Adding 1 cup white flour to this recipe will make the dough easier to handle.

Set dough aside for 20 minutes, wet hands in water, mold balls of dough the size of hens' eggs, pat into thin cakes, and bake on soapstone or lightly greased griddle, turning until brown on both sides.

TORTILLAS (2)
(With Wheat Flour)

2 cups flour   1½ teaspoons baking powder
1 teaspoon salt   1 tablespoon fat
                            cold water

Mix and sift dry ingredients, cut in the fat and add cold water to make a stiff dough, 2/3 cup. Knead on lightly floured board, make small balls, pat thin, bake on soapstone or lightly greased griddle.

(The only way to be sure of making *tortillas* correctly is to have a line of Indian ancestry running back about five hundred years.)

CRACKLING CORN BREAD

1 cup blue corn meal   3 teaspoons baking powder
1 cup flour   1½ cups sweet milk
1 teaspoon salt   1 cup home rendered
2 eggs   cracklings

Cut the fat of a hog into cubes and heat until most of the lard is rendered out, leaving the cracklings. Mix and sift dry ingredients, add milk gradually, well-beaten eggs, and cracklings. Bake in a greased pan in a hot oven about 25 minutes.

BISCOCHUELOS
(Sweet Bread)

1 cake yeast (2 in winter)	½ cup lard
2 cups luke warm water	1½ cups sugar
2 tablespoons sugar	2 eggs
6 to 7 cups flour	1 teaspoon salt
1 teaspoon anise seed	

Dissolve yeast and 2 tablespoons sugar in warm water. Stir in 3 cups flour or enough to make an ordinary sponge. Beat until mixture is smooth, and allow to rise in a warm place from 1½ to 2 hours.

Add lard and sugar creamed, eggs well beaten, salt, anise seed, and rest of flour or enough to make a moderately firm dough. Knead on floured board until smooth and elastic. Place in greased bowl, cover, and set in a warm place until light and double in bulk: about 2 hours. Knead again and let rise again: about 3 minutes.

Knead again and shape into loaves, place in greased baking tins, lightly grease tops, and let rise again until double in bulk. Bake in moderately hot oven for 10 minutes, and continue in moderate oven for 45 to 50 minutes.

The second rising may be omitted, but it helps to give a good texture to the bread. The whole process takes all day in summer, and generally two days in winter.

BOLLOS or MOLLETES
(Sweet Buns)

Follow directions for *Biscochuelos*. After second rising mold into small round buns and place in well-greased pan. Cover and let rise until double in bulk, and a slight depression remains when pressed with the finger: about 1 hour.

Brush lightly with melted lard or butter, and put a lump of *piloncillo* or brown sugar on each bun. Bake in moderately hot oven for 20 to 25 minutes.

These were served with chocolate or coffee in this form or split and toasted, covered with butter, sugar and cinnamon, and reheated.

BUÑUELOS or SOPAIPILLAS
(Fried Puffs)

2 eggs
1 cup milk

¾ teaspoon salt
1 teaspoon baking powder
4 cups flour

Sift dry ingredients together. Beat eggs well, add milk, and stir in dry ingredients, adding as much flour as it will absorb.

Roll as thin as possible, cut and fry in deep fat until a delicate golden brown. Cut into small squares, they make *sopaipillas*. Cut large and round and with a hole pinched in the middle, they make *buñuelos*.

They were served with Mexican chocolate at four in the afternoon.

Served with the following sauce, *buñuelos* were used as a dessert.

Sauce for Buñuelos

6 tablespoons *piloncillo*
½ cup water

½ cup wine
½ cup seeded raisins
½ teaspoon cinnamon

Combine ingredients and boil until it begins to thicken. Pour over hot *buñuelos* and serve at once.

Cakes and Cookies

EMPANADAS
(Turn-Overs)

2 cups flour
1/3 cup milk
1 teaspoon baking powder

½ teaspoon salt
½ cup lard
1 pinch *culantro*

Mix and sift dry ingredients. Cut in the lard, and add the moisture. Roll out to ⅛ inch thickness, and cut into 4-inch circles.

Fill with fruit mixture, moisten edges with cold water, fold one half over the other and press edges together. Fry in deep fat until brown, and drain on brown paper.

Empanadas were filled with various mixtures. The imagination may go on forever, making new combinations. Mincemeat makes a very desirable filling.

The favorites were probably:

(1)

1 cup pumpkin	½ cup sugar
½ cup raisins	½ teaspoon each, cloves
½ cup *piñones* or almonds	and allspice

Prepare pumpkin as for vegetable, or use canned pumpkin. Rub through a colander and add other ingredients.

(2)

1 cup boiled **tongue,** finely chopped	1 cup raisins
½ cup *piñones* or shredded almonds	½ cup sugar
½ cup wine	½ teaspoon cinnamon
	¼ teaspoon each cloves and allspice

½ teaspoon cinnamon

Mix all ingredients well and brown in oven, stirring to brown evenly. Add meat stock if mixture seems too dry.

(3)

½ cup boiled pork
½ cup dried cooked
  apricots
¼ teaspoon each, cloves
  and allspice

½ cup sugar
½ teaspoon cinnamon
½ cup raisins and
  currants, mixed
½ cup shredded almonds

½ cup meat stock.

Finish as Number 2.

Canned fruits may be substituted for dried fruit.

Empanadas were always made at Christmas time and served between meals with wine.

BISCOCHITOS (1)
(Cookies)

2 cups butter or lard
½ cup boiling water
1 teaspoon baking powder
1¼ cups sugar

4 cups flour
½ teaspoon salt
¼ cup whisky
1 teaspoon anise seed

Melt the shortening in the hot water, add whisky, sugar, anise seed. Sift together 2 cups flour, baking powder, and salt. Stir all together and add enough remaining flour to make a soft dough. Roll on a floured board about ⅛ inch thick, cut with a floured cookie cutter, place on cookie tins, brush with melted butter, sprinkle with sugar and cinnamon, and bake in a moderately hot oven until brown: about 10 minutes. Old cooks fold them like a fleur de lis.

BISCOCHITOS (2)

1 pound sugar   4 oz. cinnamon
1 pound flour   1 pound lard
1 dozen egg yolks

Sift cinnamon, sugar, and flour together. Add to cold lard the yolks of the eggs, then add dry ingredients, mix well, and mold into balls the size of a marble and flatten. Place on buttered tins, about 1 inch apart. Bake about 6 minutes in a moderate oven. While still hot sprinkle with powdered sugar and cinnamon.

PASTELITOS

1 pound dried apricots
  (2½ cups fruit pulp) 3 teaspoons sugar
1¼ cups sugar   1 teaspoon cinnamon

Use pastel recipe given on page 85.

Wash dried apricots and soak overnight, or for several hours. Cook until soft enough to press through colander or ricer or mash well. (If mashed, pulp contains the skins and less dried fruit need be cooked.) Add sugar to pulp and cook until very thick. Let cool.

Roll out one half the pastry large enough to line a baking sheet. Spread fruit mixture on this and cover with other half of pastry. Press edges together. Sprinkle with mixture of sugar and cinnamon. Mark in small squares before baking, and prick each square with fork.

Bake in hot oven about 20 minutes. Cool and cut as marked.

Pastelitos should be about as thick as the little finger. Any kind of dried fruit or combination of dried fruits may be used. Raisins may be added to the apricot pulp.

This makes about 35 *pastelitos.*

QUESADILLAS (1)

1 ¾ cups fresh goats' cheese   ⅛ teaspoon salt
  (¼ cake)   pastry (see page 85)
          ½ cup sugar

Grind cheese, add sugar and salt, and mix well.

Roll out one half the pastry thin and lay on baking sheet. Spread the cheese mixture on this and cover with other half the pastry. Press edges together. Brush over with melted lard or milk and sprinkle with sugar. Mark into small squares and prick each square with a fork.

Bake in moderate oven until brown, about 20 minutes.

Cool and cut as marked.

These *quesadillas* may be shaped as in recipe 2.

QUESADILLAS (2)

1 cup *requeson* or cottage cheese

2 eggs

½ cup sugar

⅛ teaspoon salt

⅛ teaspoon cinnamon

½ cup dried currants (if desired)

Pastry

Mash cheese, add well-beaten eggs, sugar, salt, and cinnamon.

Roll pastry into thin sheets and cut into 4-inch squares. Place 1 tablespoon cheese mixture on half of each square. Moisten edges, fold over other half, making a triangle. Press edges together and prick with a fork. Brush over with melted lard or milk, sprinkle with sugar, and bake in a moderate oven until brown, about 20 minutes.

Cheese

GOATS' MILK CHEESE

1 gallon fresh goats' milk   1 junket or rennet tablet

Crush the tablet and add to luke-warm milk. Allow to stand in a warm place until a solid clabber is formed. Stir, put into a cheesecloth bag, and allow to hang until all the whey drains from it. Mold into a ball or flat cake. It may be served with cream and sugar or syrup.

Or slice and sprinkle with sugar. Brown lightly in a moderate oven and serve with milk and sugar.

RESQUESONES
(Whey Cheese)

Put whey on the stove, allowing it to boil slowly from one side of the vessel only. Pour into it, ½ cup at a time, sweet milk. As curd forms, dip it into a strainer covered with cheesecloth, and set aside to drain. It makes a very delicate cheese.

If seasoning is desired, add ¼ teaspoon salt to cheese made from each quart of milk.

The whey may be used several times. Whey from goats' milk cheese is excellent.

Candies and Preserves

MELCOCHA
(Molasses Candy)

2 cups molasses or
   dark syrup
1 cup *piloncillo*

1 tablespoon vinegar
2 tablespoons butter
½ tablespoon anise seed

Mix molasses, *piloncillo*, vinegar, and butter. Cook slowly until sugar is dissolved; then boil until brittle when dropped into cold water. Pour into a buttered pan and sprinkle with anise seed. When cool enough to handle and beginning to harden, pull until stiff and light. Twist into sticks flattened at each end.

DULCE DE CALABAZA
(Pumpkin Sweet)

1 squash, fully ripe but not yellow	1 pound sugar for each pound squash
½ tablespoon lime water	1 gallon water
1 pinch *culantro*	

Cut squash into strips 2 by 4 inches, removing seeds.

Prepare a mild lye by boiling lime in water, stir until it stops bubbling and allow to settle. When clear, pour it over the squash, enough to cover, and let it stand all night.

In the morning remove squash from lye and wash in clear water until all the taste of lye is gone. Then boil in fresh water until tender, but not soft. Drop at once into ice-cold water, and drain.

Boil sugar and water 10 minutes, add squash and *culantro* and boil slowly in a covered vessel until the syrup is thick, and the squash well-done. The syrup should be clear and the squash brittle.

This will keep several weeks in a cool place.

DULCE DE PILONCILLO
(Brown Sugar Candy)

2 cups crushed *piloncillo*   1 tablespoon butter
   or brown sugar   ½ cup water or milk
1 tablespoon vinegar   1 cup *piñones*
       few drops bitter almond extract

Mix sugar, water, vinegar, and butter, and boil until syrup threads when dropped from a spoon. Add a few drops of almond extract, cool slightly, add *piñones* and beat until creamy. Drop from tip of spoon on oiled paper or pour into a buttered pan and cut into squares.

Pecans may be substituted for *piñones*.

GREEN FIG PRESERVES

Select figs that are green and very hard. Prepare a mild lye solution as directed for *Dulce de Calabaza*. Make a small slit in the blossom end of each fig, and boil them in the lye solution until tender. Drain, drop in ice water, and leave overnight. In the morning, squeeze the water out of each fig and wash until the taste of lye has entirely disappeared.

For each cup of figs, make the following syrup:

1 cup sugar   ½ cup water

Boil sugar and water for 10 minutes, add figs and cook until tender. A piece of ginger root one inch long may be added for flavor.

This preserve will keep indefinitely if sealed in jars when hot.

CAJETA DE MEMBRILLO
(Quince Butter)

1 cup quince   1 cup sugar

Peel and quarter two large ripe quinces. Add enough water to cover and boil slowly until soft. Rub through a colander, add sugar and cook slowly until the bottom of the kettle can be seen when stirring, about 1 hour. Stir occasionally to prevent burning. Pour into individual molds. When it hardens, it is ready to use.

Serve with meats.

Beverages

MISTELA DE CHIMAJÁ
(Christmas Drink)

1 gallon whisky	1 pound sugar
1 quart water	4 sticks cinnamon
2 cups dried *chimajá* root	1 whole dried orange peel

(Orange peel must be very dry; otherwise a bitter taste will result.)

Boil sugar, cinnamon, orange peel, *chimajá* root, and water for ½ hour. Strain and add whisky. After two weeks the drink is ready, but it improves steadily with age. It attains about the consistency of a liqueur. It was the inevitable Christmas drink.

Some recipes call for no boiling. The ingredients were mixed and set aside in a jug which was shaken well each day for two weeks. The liqueur was then drained off and was ready.

CHOCOLATE (1)

6 squares Mexican chocolate
6 cups milk   yolk of 1 egg

   Grate or cut the chocolate into small pieces, and dissolve in ½ cup scalded milk. Add the rest of the milk, bring slowly to the boil and boil about 5 minutes. Beat the egg in a bowl, and continue beating while pouring in the hot chocolate. Return to the fire and bring again to the boil, beating with *molino* or egg beater. Beat to a froth before serving each cup.

CHOCOLATE (2)

2 squares chocolate grated   1 cup cream
½ cup boiling water   few grains salt
2 cups milk   pinch nutmeg and allspice
3 tablespoons sugar   1 teaspoon cinnamon
1 teaspoon vanilla   1 egg

   Boil chocolate in water for 5 minutes. Add milk, cream, sugar, salt, spices. Cook in top of double boiler an hour, beating vigorously at 5 to 10 minute intervals.

QUICK CHOCOLATE

4 cups milk
½ cup boiling water
1½ squares chocolate
2 tablespoons sugar
¼ teaspoon cinnamon

⅛ teaspoon nutmeg
few grains salt
¼ teaspoon almond
  extract or ½ teaspoon
  vanilla

5 marshmallows

Scald milk, boil chocolate, sugar, spices, and salt in water for 5 minutes, add scalded milk, add marshmallows and beat until they are dissolved. Reheat and add extract. Beat until foamy.

CHAMPURRADO

Add to the *Atole* recipe,* 2 squares of Mexican chocolate, sweetened to taste, 1 to 1½ cups sugar. Dissolve chocolate in the boiling salted water, add the moistened meal and sugar, and continue as for *Atole*.

If Mexican chocolate is not available, substitute 1½ squares chocolate, ⅛ teaspoon nutmeg, and ¼ teaspoon cinnamon.

See page 16

Comidas

(1)   *Cream of Pea Soup*
Chiles Rellenos
Carne de Marrano y Chile   *Mexican Rice*
Lettuce with French Dressing
Custard
Coffee

(2)   *Albóndigas Soup*
Pollo con Arroz
Quelites   *Dried Peas*
Guacamole
Fruit in Syrup   *Biscochitos*
Coffee

(3)   *Plain Bean Soup*
Carne Adobada (roasted)
Frijoles
Elegante or Quelites
Crackling Corn Bread
Natillas
Coffee

(4)   *Cream of Corn Soup*
Spanish Roast
Macaroni con Chile   *Quince Marmalade*
Lettuce and Tomato Salad
Tortillas
Empanadas
Coffee

(5)   *Chiles Rellenos con Queso or Enchiladas*
   Chile con Carne   *Frijoles*
                            Tortillas
                         Avocada Salad
                         Fruit Pastel
                            Coffee

(6)   *Ostiones*
   Pollo Relleno   *Spanish Rice*
                         Capirotada
                         Almendrado
                            Coffee

(7)   *CHRISTMAS DINNER*
Caldo Colado
Suckling Pig
with dressing and red apple in mouth
Turkey or Chicken, roasted
Rice served with hard-boiled eggs
Stewed Tomatoes   *Tortillas*
Wine
Chopped Lettuce Salad with French Dressing
Buñuelos with Spiced Syrup
Coffee

INDEX